THE FARM

An American Living Portrait

Joan and David Hagan

1469 Morstein Road, West Chester, Pennsylvania 19380

Main entrance way

We dedicate this book to Mr. and Mrs.
William D. Hagan, Mr. and Mrs. John
Jakum, Patricia A. Hagan and David H.
Hagan, Jr.

Published by Schiffer Publishing, Ltd.
1469 Morstein Road
West Chester, Pennsylania 19380
Please write for a free catalog
This book may be purchased from the publisher.
Please include $2.00 postage.
Try your bookstore first.

Printed in the United States of America.
ISBN: 0-88740-257-7

Introduction

In the spring, the smell of fresh plowed ground and the sight of new growth on nearby orchards makes us all feel young and fresh again. The sounds of birds busy gathering materials for their nest aad the bellowing of dairy cows turned out for the first time since winter, announce the arrival of spring.

Farming anywhere in the world is always of great interest, but is too often taken for granted. Farming is the foundation from which our basic needs for survival come. The dedication, commitment and hard work of our farmers is a heritage we can all be proud of.

From state to state and county to county, we have found barns of many shapes and sizes. It seems there are no two alike. The different designs and innovations are a tribute to the basics of necessity. Outside colors and decorative trim in the wood work varies from very plain to very ornate. The surrounding toolsheds, smoke houses, spring houses and outhouses all have their own personalities.

On every farm we visited we could find much of its past still present. Chestnut pegged beams, old horseshoes and horse collars hanging in their place told of a time not too long ago. The dinner bells standing sildent in the yards can almost still be heard ringing out for dinner or an emergency. The old hand gas pumps covered with rust, cracked and pealing paint tell of the early days of the gas powered machines and their beginning in farming. The old log tobacco barns in North Carolina have all but disappeared.

The smiles of the people reflect the life in which they live. The wonderful character lines in their faces and their calloused hands show their love for the land. We cannot say enough kind words about the new friends we have made or the feelings they shared with us.

This collection of images is intended to make us all slow down and reflect on a time when things seemed much simpler.

Spring, 1990   Joan and David Hagan

2-hole corn sheller

Skylight.

ROCK HALL, MARYLAND

HARTLEY, DELAWARE

Amish dairy barn and wagon shed.

Milk cans in cooling tank.

Milk cans are drying out.

Corn crib.

Water tower.

Milk can lids in drying rack.

Running horse weather vane, Guilford, Maine.

Following page:
Weathered dairy barn in Guilford, Maine.

GUILFORD, MAINE

Stone end barn in Rising Sun, Maryland.

RISING SUN, MARYLAND

Bank barn in Rising Sun, Maryland.

Out house.

Hand water pump.

Kitten peeks out under the door of tool shed.

Horse farm in Monkton, Maryland.

Bank barn in Monkton, Maryland.

MONKTON, MARYLAND

Stone horse stable in Monkton, Maryland.
Maze of fence in Monkton, Maryland.

Dairy barn, creamery and loading shoot.

Back view of dairy barn in Elkton, Maryland.

ELKTON, MARYLAND

MONKTON, MARYLAND

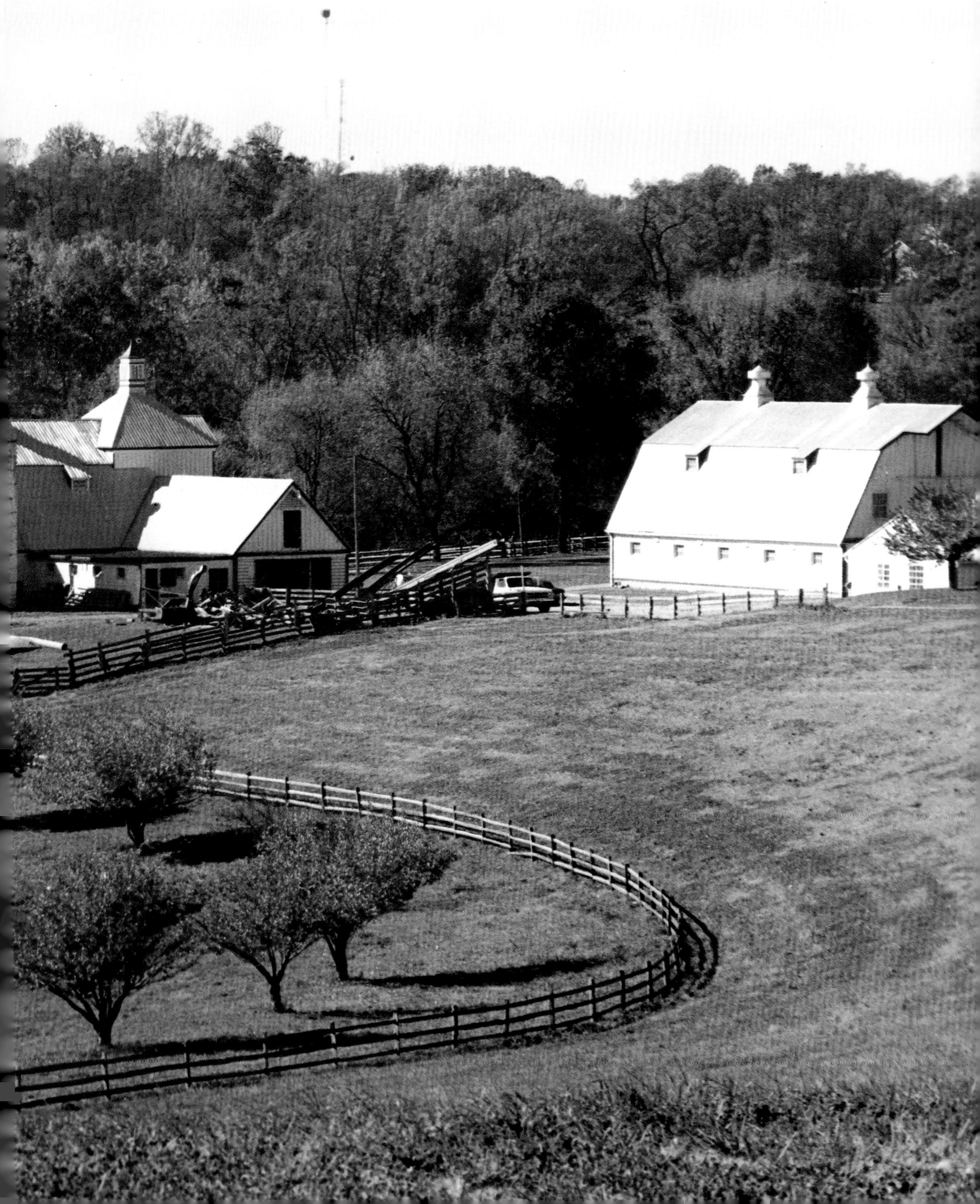

Bank barn in Rising Sun, Maryland.

Stables of stone.

Tulips are a sign of spring.

RISING SUN, MARYLAND

Stone end barn.

Dairy barn built in 1940.

Farmer with old friend.

Door latches to stable.

HARFORD COUNTY, MARYLAND

Preceding page:
Rolling hills of Harford County, Maryland.
Opposite page:
Bank barn.
Wash house.

Worton, Maryland.

Corn crib.

WORTON, MARYLAND

Rooster weather vane.

Door on corn crib.

ROCK HALL, MARYLAND.

My horses are all over 20 years old.
Heading to the pasture to mow.

Bank Barn in Phoenix, Maryland.
Window in loft.

Spring house.

PHOENIX, MARYLAND

Natures second crop in Kennedyville, Maryland.

Floyd Price with part of fall crop in Kennedyville, Maryland.

Kennedyville, Maryland hay barn raising.

Gas powered nail gun works great.

Floyd gets helpful advice.

Settling the first truss.

Finished just in time.

Running the stringers.
Time to knock off.

Monkton, Maryland.
Hand pump still works.

Close inspection.

MONKTON, MARYLAND

Cecilton, Maryland.

Patterns in wood.

Ice house.

Brown Swiss are curious.

ACCIDENT, MARYLAND
Hand shock corn in Accident, Maryland.

Old split rail fence in Western Maryland.

Stone spring house in Accident, Maryland.

Accident, Maryland.

Old road bed in Western Maryland.

Brick end bank barn in Lineboro, Maryland.

LINEBORO, MARYLAND

Bank barn in Lineboro, Maryland.

Lineboro, Maryland.

Barn and grainery on right.

Nap time!

GLEN ROCK, PENNSYLVANIA

FREDERICK, MARYLAND

Dairy barn in Frederick, Maryland.

Carriage house in Frederick, Maryland.

Never to run again.

Frederick, Maryland.

Westminster, Maryland.

Smoke house.

Grainery in Westminster, Maryland.

Opposite page: Billy goats bluff.

WESTMINSTER, MARYLAND

Bank barn in Westminster, Maryland.

Log spring house in Westminster, Maryland.

Copula.

Airator window

"Big" dog house.

Opposite page:
OAKLAND, MARYLAND
Fall pasture.

Smoke house.

Bank barn, White Hall, Maryland.

Scotts Highland.

Spring house.

WHITE HALL, MARYLAND

Scotts Highland bull.

OAKLAND, MARYLAND

Brick end barn.

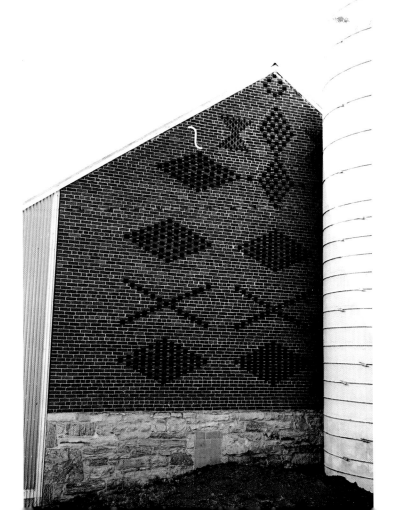

Following page:
CHURCHVILLE, MARYLAND

CLEAR SPRING, MARYLAND

OAKLAND, MARYLAND

Too cold to come out.

NORRISVILLE, MARYLAND

Silo

Copulas

CHURCHVILLE, MARYLAND

Indian Head Farms, Churchville, Maryland.

Tobacco barns in Fuquay-Varina, North Carolina.

Tobacco sticks.

Hand dug well.

Previous page:
FUQUAY-VARINA, NORTH CAROLINA

FUQUAY-VARINA, NORTH CAROLINA

Angier, North Carolina.

Tobacco in ready for market.

Tobacco sticks.

Happy farm boy.

Log tobacco barn 100 years old, Oxford, North Carolina.

OXFORD, NORTH CAROLINA

Smoke house.

Red rooster bank barn in Stewartstown, Pennsylvania.

Copulas.

Spring house.

Copula.

Canada Geese.

WEST CHESTER, PENNSYLVANIA

Peter's pig.

Spring house, West Chester, Pennsylvania.

Copula with rooster weather vane.

COCHRANVILLE, PENNSYLVANIA

Well kept stables.

Pegged beams.

#1 mouse trap in the barn.

YORK COUNTY, PENNSYLVANIA

Watch dog.

LITTLESTOWN, PENNSYLVANIA

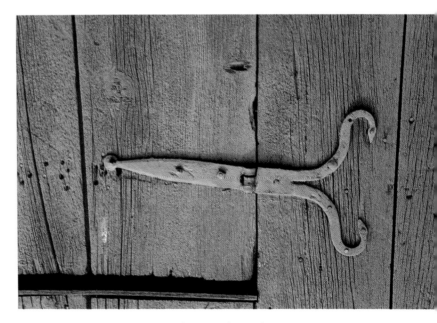

Hinge on barn door.

Latch on smoke house.

Spring house in Littlestown, Pennsylvania.

Smoke house.

Hinge on smoke house.

Bank Barn, Littlestown, Pennsylvania.

Bank barn, Brodbecks, Pennsylvania.

Builders name and date.

Door latch with lock.

BRODBECKS, PENNSYLVANIA

Round barn with silo in middle. Located in Biglerville,
Pennsylvania.

Silo.

BIGLERVILLE, PENNSYLVANIA

Spring house on left, smoke house on right.

Spring.

Copula.

Barn in Littlestown, Pennsylvania.

Copula.

Spring house.

Cooling off!

STEWARTSTOWN, PENNSYLVANIA

Bank barn in Littlestown, Pennsylvania.

Copula.

LITTLESTOWN, PENNSYLVANIA

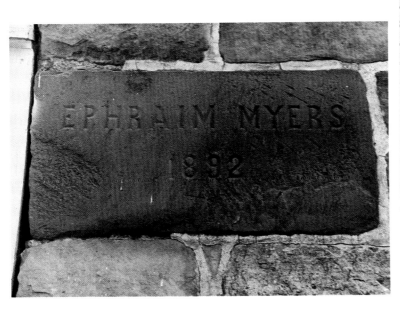

GLEN ROCK, PENNSYLVANIA

Brick end barn in Glen Rock, Pennsylvania.

Wheat sheaves and diamonds.

Bank barn.

Stables.

BIRD IN HAND, PENNSYLVANIA

Bank barn.

Heading to the hay field with team.

Father and son bail hay.

Wife rakes hay.

Hooking up the team.

Lots of work to do.

Pheasant weather vane.

Smoke house.

STEWARTSTOWN, PENNSYLVANIA

GARDENVILLE, PENNSYLVANIA
Amish farm in Gardenville, Pennsylvania.

Tobacco basket hangs on side of barn.

Following page:
Wood shed with tobacco basket at top.

VIRGILINA, VIRGINIA

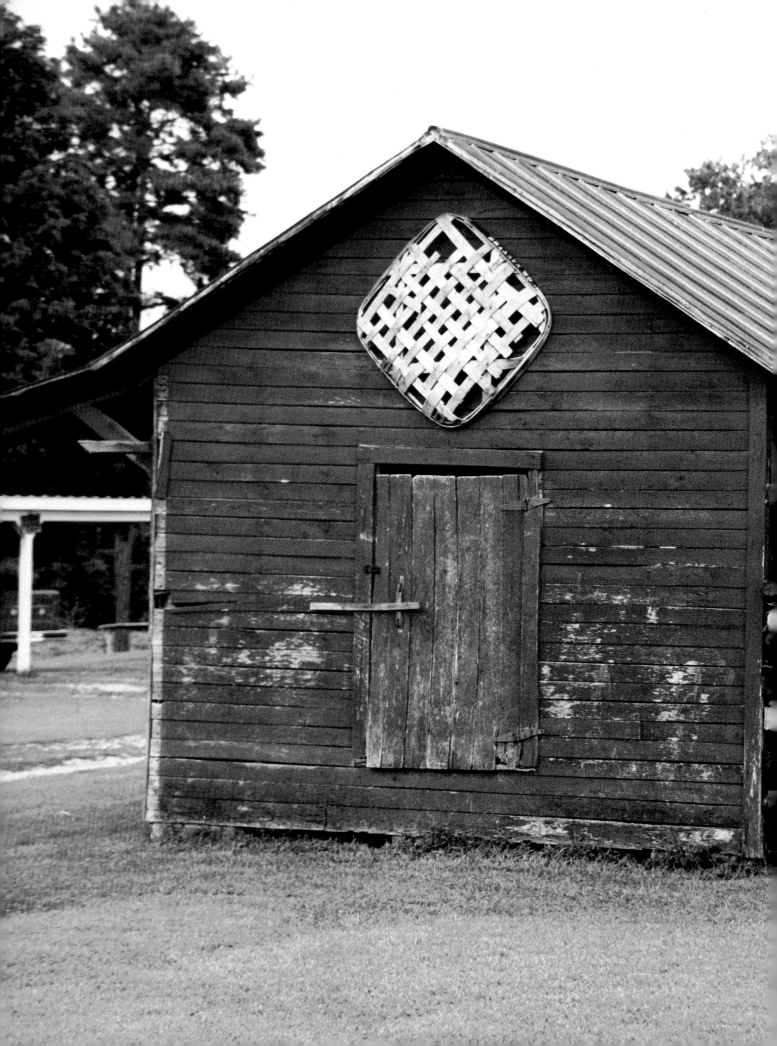

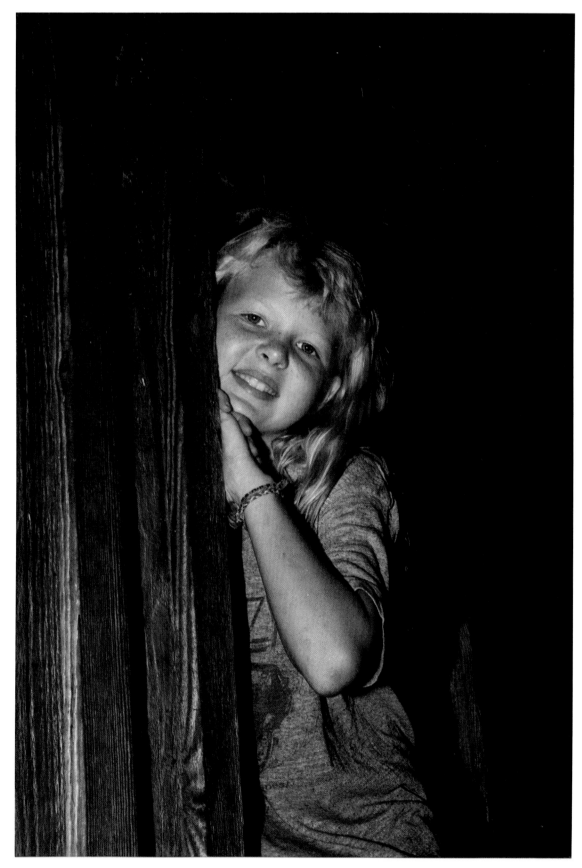

"Virginia Miss"

Eight-sided barn in Madison, Virginia.

MADISON, VIRGINIA

Wash and spring house.

Goodies in the root cellar.

Out house.

Following page:
Relaxing evening on farm pond.

QUEENSTOWN, MARYLAND

Smoke house and dinner bell.

''The more mold the better the ham''.

CECIL COUNTY, MARYLAND

KENT COUNTY, MARYLAND